BREATHE
out

BREATHE out

A CREATIVE GUIDE TO HAPPINESS FOR TEEN MINDS

In aid of

All royalties from the sale of this book (a minimum of £7,500) will be donated to Mind, a registered charity in England and Wales (charity number 219830).

Michael O'Mara Books Limited

First published in Great Britain in 2020
by Michael O'Mara Books Limited
9 Lion Yard
Tremadoc Road
London SW4 7NQ

A CIP catalogue record for this book is available from the British Library.

Papers used by Michael O'Mara Books Limited are natural, recyclable
products made from wood grown in sustainable forests. The manufacturing
processes conform to the environmental regulations of the country of origin.

ISBN: 978-1-78929-262-6 in paperback print format

4 5 6 7 8 9 10

www.mombooks.com

Illustrated by Celeste Wallaert
Written by Fiona Slater
Designed by Ana Bjezancevic and Barbara Ward

Every reasonable effort has been made to acknowledge all copyright holders.
Any errors or omissions that may have occurred are inadvertent, and anyone
with any copyright queries is invited to write to the publisher, so that full
acknowledgement may be included in subsequent editions of the work.

Printed and bound in China by Leo Paper Products

MIX
Paper from
responsible sources
FSC® C020056

This journal belongs to:

_____

_____

Breathe Out is published by Michael O'Mara Books
to raise money and awareness for Mind, the mental
health charity. All royalties from the sale of this book
(a minimum of £7,500) will be donated to Mind,
a registered charity in England (no. 219830) and
a registered company (no. 424348) in England and Wales.

Mind believes that no one should have to face a mental
health problem alone. We're here for you. Today. Now.
We're on your doorstep, at the end of the phone or online.
Whether you're stressed, depressed or in crisis, we'll listen,
give support and advice and fight your corner.

For information on how to contact Mind, see the
'Resources' section near the back of the book.

CONTENTS

INTRODUCTION

What does happiness mean to you? Happiness can be a feeling that we experience for a time and it can also be something closer to a lasting state of contentment. It can be wildly exciting or more low-key. The truth is that people have been debating the meaning of happiness for centuries and we're still working on it today.

The exercises in this book are designed to help you discover your own sense of what happiness means, how it feels to you personally, and how to build more of it into your life.

Of course, there are a lot of myths around happiness. For example, we're often told that certain things *should* make us happy – it might be success, more possessions, smaller/bigger/taller/shorter [insert body part here]. If we can just look and live like those sparkly smiley people on social media we'll be happy, because they're happy, right? But it doesn't tend to work that way.

Equally, no one can be happy all the time. That's just not how we're made. There are going to be times when we will feel down, worried, upset, angry and all the other emotions that we come pre-programmed with. It's part of being human. And all these myths, such as the idea that certain things should make us happy or that we ought to be happy all the time, can actually make us less happy as we chase impossible goals, meanwhile feeling like there's something wrong with us. But there is another way. By getting to know ourselves better and acknowledging our experiences we can make room for more happiness in our lives – whether that's the euphoric, joyful kind, the more stable, peaceful kind, or a bit of both.

As you go through the book, you might find that some exercises speak to you more than others. Feel free to dip in and out, and go with what works for you.

HOW DO YOU SEE YOU?

Write your name in the bubble opposite. Now start noting down words that you associate with yourself. Think of 'I am ...' or 'I am someone who ...' For example, you might write 'I am resourceful' or 'I am someone who cares about others'.

Once you have a few ideas written down, have a think about how you feel about each one of them. Which ones make you stand tall? Which push you down or hold you back? Did you always believe them about yourself? Where might these labels have come from?

You probably won't know all the answers (and you don't need to!). The idea here is to start getting a sense of how you think about yourself and how these beliefs affect you. It might feel like some of them are set in stone – 'it's just how I am', kind of statements – but it's likely that they're more flexible than they seem. You weren't born with these labels and you get to choose which ones you accept.

PEN. PAPER. SIMPLE.

Pick up pen.

●

Place tip of pen on page near arrow.

●

Move it.

●

Keep moving it.

●

That's it.

Yes, that really is it. It doesn't matter if you recreate the Mona Lisa or doodle curious shapes that remind you of your dog. You could plaster the whole page in a colour or scribble intricate patterns in the corners. This isn't about creating art or unlocking the secrets of your inner world. It's about making marks on paper. Because, sometimes, that's all it takes to give your mind a break, helping you to release a bit of what you're experiencing on the inside and feel calmer.

FOCUS

You'll find quite a few exercises in this book that ask you to focus your attention on a particular thing for a given amount of time. But the skill of focussing – training our attention to stay where we want it – is one that takes practice. This exercise is designed to help you improve that skill, and also works as a useful mindfulness technique.

1. Get as comfortable as you can.

2. Begin by focussing your attention on the sound of your breath flowing in and out – it can help if you close your eyes. Give yourself time to really listen.

3. Now extend your attention beyond your breathing. What other sounds do you notice?

4. Pick one out and again focus your attention on it.

5. When you're ready, reach out with your attention once more and select a new sound.

6. Continue to pick out and focus on sounds in this way for about 5–10 minutes or as long as you can manage or find helpful. You'll probably be surprised by how many different sources of sound you can distinguish.

7. When your attention wanders (and it normally does), notice this, too, and gently bring it back to the sound.

TIP

You can also do this focussing exercise using your other senses. For example, you could use touch, focussing your attention on the feel of an object in your hands or the textures of the different clothes that you're wearing.

THE STORIES WE TELL OURSELVES

Right now, in your head, you're hard at work on your autobiography. And you're the only reader.

In fact, we're all doing it. As we innocently go about our day, a part of our mind is busy making notes, spinning stories about our life and our place in it. Maybe you've noticed it: a quiet narrator commenting on what you've done, how you've handled something, how you sounded, how you looked...

What does your narrator say about you? If you mess up, is it 'failed again, stupid!' or 'ah well, better luck next time'? When you achieve something does it cheer you on? More generally, what kind of story are you telling yourself? Is it a heart-warming tale or a cold, critical review?

Over the next week try to listen out for that narrator, tune in to what it's saying about you and, crucially, how it makes you feel. If it gets negative try to swap it for a supportive alternative – think about what you might say to a good friend.

Sometimes, because we've heard them so often, we can believe that the stories we tell ourselves are facts. But the reality is that you're the author; you get to the write the story. It takes practice and most of all compassion, but offering yourself kindness and encouragement can have a significant impact on how you feel about yourself.

TIP

Give your internal narrator a pen name. It can help you recognize it and treat it with more detachment. A few suggestions to start you off: Drama Kitten, Brain Noodle, Bulldozer, Dave (unless you're called Dave).

PRACTICE COMPASSION

Speaking kindly to yourself can take practice when you're not used to it. Here are some ideas of things you could say to get you started:

- I'm allowed to make mistakes.

- I can't be perfect. No one is. And I don't need to be.

- My feelings matter.

- My feelings are valid.

It's important that you believe the things you say to yourself. For example, you might not truly believe that you are allowed to make mistakes. So instead you could start smaller, with something that acknowledges what it's like to be you in this moment. It could be something like, 'when I make a mistake I find it really hard – it's understandable'. Have a think now about what might work for you and record your ideas here. What could you say to yourself that is kind and gentle?

_____

_____

_____

_____

_____

_____

_____

_____

_____

_____

_____

TIP

If you find it difficult to change the tone of how you speak to yourself try not to beat yourself up. Changing habits like these can be really tough – and that's actually worth acknowledging and being kind about too!

CREATE YOUR OWN SELF-CARE TOOLKIT

Use the opposite page to plan the contents of your own personalized self-care kit – something you can open up any time you're a little down or you feel like you need to recharge your batteries. Some ideas for what you could include are:

- Fluffy socks
- A favourite book or poem
- Tasty snacks
- Toys or trinkets from childhood

- Photos of you and your friends
- A bath bomb
- A face mask
- Herbal tea

WHAT MATTERS TO YOU?

What are your values? These are qualities and principles that matter to you deeply. They aren't things that you feel you *should* be or have been told are important, rather things that inspire you personally.

On the opposite page, circle the values that matter most to you.

Are there any missing? Write them down at the bottom of the page.

Keeping our values in mind as we make decisions, set goals, interact with others (and ourselves – self-care is always an important practice, people!) and generally go about our day, means that even the small stuff can add up, boosting self-esteem, confidence and our sense of fulfilment.

TIP

Our values can change over time so you could try this exercise again in a year to see what's different.

CURIOSITY	ADAPTABILITY	RESPECT
CARING	SPIRITUALITY	CREATIVITY
FRIENDSHIP	RESILIENCE	COOPERATION
ADVENTURE	PATIENCE	LOYALTY
RELIABILITY	SELF RESPECT	LOVE
FORGIVENESS	FAMILY	KINDNESS
FUN	GRATITUDE	KNOWLEDGE
AUTHENTICITY	GENEROSITY	HUMOUR
BRAVERY	FAIRNESS	
ACCEPTANCE	EXCITEMENT	
FREEDOM	OPEN-MINDEDNESS	
WISDOM	CHALLENGE	

LISTEN OUT FOR THE GOOD

We've all got a limited amount of attention and what we spend it on can influence our mood across the day. Sometimes we need to remind ourselves to pay attention to the good stuff: good stuff that's happening around us and also good stuff about us. It's about listening out for the positives, noticing when someone tells us, 'nice work' or even just, 'thank you', acknowledging the part you played in achievements and allowing yourself to be proud of that.

When we're feeling down or focussed on just getting through the day, it can become all too easy to let the good stuff pass us by, especially if we have a habit of spending our attention on the negatives.

This isn't about ignoring bad experiences or putting a positive spin on them. This is about making sure that we aren't missing or dismissing the good things when they happen.

Can you list some positive experiences from the past week? Or perhaps try and remind yourself of this perspective over the course of the day or week and see what you start to notice. You could keep a log here of what comes up.

- _____
- _____

- _____
- _____

- _____
- _____

- _____
- _____

- _____
- _____

- _____

TIP

Remember, some negativity is totally
normal, but it doesn't have to be
your best friend.

THE FULL SPECTRUM

Being human means we experience a whole range of emotions. It's one of the reasons that we're at the top of the species pile. They can help us connect with one another, and tell us about what we need. Put simply, our feelings are important and if we give them some attention we can learn a lot about what makes us tick and live happier lives.

The first step is identification: to understand your feelings, it helps if you can name them. That might seem easy – you know when you're happy, sad and so on, right? But sometimes our words don't always do justice to what we're experiencing. For example, you might say that you're upset. But what does 'upset' mean to you? To one person it might be about being sad, to another it might be more about feeling lonely, frustrated or angry. It might mean all of these things at the same time. That word 'upset' can mask a lot of useful information.

Having the words to be able to express how we're feeling accurately helps us to acknowledge our experiences and recognize our needs. This exercise is all about getting to grips with that vocabulary.

Choose one of the words on the opposite page and focus on it. Do you have a sense of what it's like to experience that feeling? Is it familiar or alien to you? What other words do you associate with it? Now repeat the process with the other words on the page. Are there words missing? Write them down in the gaps.

- HAPPY
- HOPEFUL
- INVISIBLE
- JOYFUL
- SAD
- ANGRY
- FURIOUS
- ASHAMED
- MOODY
- SMALL
- STUPID
- EXCITED
- CALM
- CONFIDENT
- FRUSTRATED
- LONELY
- VULNERABLE
- CONTENT
- GUILTY

TUNE IN

Use as many words as you can to describe how you're feeling right now. Use sentences if single words aren't doing the job. Feel free to fill the page. Get more paper. Keep going!

You don't have to stick with the words on the previous pages, and you don't have to use the classic 'emotions' either. They could be more descriptive words like soft or edgy, blue or orange, squiggly or meh. As long as those words mean something to you, they belong here.

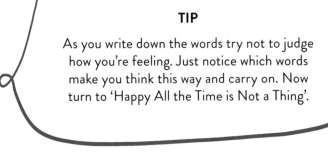

TIP

As you write down the words try not to judge how you're feeling. Just notice which words make you think this way and carry on. Now turn to 'Happy All the Time is Not a Thing'.

HAPPY ALL THE TIME IS NOT A THING

No one is happy all the time. Not one single person. Ever. We're just not designed that way.

The weird thing is that despite this fact of life we're surrounded by messages, from our social media feeds, in advertising, on TV, all telling us that we ought to be happy 24/7, and if you're not, it may make you feel as if you're doing something wrong.

When we're surrounded by messages like this we can easily start to believe them. We can begin to feel as if we shouldn't feel what we feel, that our feelings are wrong. Sure, some feelings can be uncomfortable and painful, we may not enjoy feeling them, but there is never anything wrong with them.

But when we think that we shouldn't feel a certain way we can find ourselves struggling against those feelings – by trying to squash them down, ignoring them or putting on a brave face. We try and force ourselves to be happy and if we can't be happy we might want to try and 'fake it 'til we make it'.

This can cause us problems and actually have the opposite effect. If we struggle against our emotions it can interfere with that flow. Also, if we ignore them rather than listening to them we're missing out on important information about how we can help ourselves (flip back to 'The Full Spectrum' for more ideas on this).

It's not that you shouldn't do things to cheer yourself up when you're down, more that you shouldn't judge yourself about being down in the first place. Try not to think about emotions as being good or bad in themselves – there's a spectrum for a very good reason, after all.

The next time you find yourself beginning to struggle take it as an opportunity to tune in and take care of yourself. The exercise on the following page is a good place to start.

HOW MUCH IS A PICTURE WORTH AGAIN?

Words are not the only way that you can express your feelings. Doing something creative, such as drawing or making a model, can also be really effective.

Use these pages to draw how you're feeling. Think about the colours, the shapes, where on the page you want to draw. The end result can be as random and abstract as you like. These are your feelings!

TIP

For more ideas of other creative ways to express yourself, flip forward to 'Make Something' on page 83.

A MINDFUL APPROACH

Put simply, mindfulness is about consciously paying full attention to the present moment – to your thoughts and feelings, and what's going on around you – with an attitude of acceptance, compassion and curiosity. By focusing on what's happening with you right now you can observe your thoughts and feelings and choose how to respond.

Mindfulness can reduce the symptoms of feeling low, worried or angry. It can also improve concentration and even help with exam performance.

You can practice mindfulness by following specific meditations (there are a few in this book, such as 'Being With Your Feelings') or there are apps that you can use, but you can also bring a mindful approach into your life more generally by paying extra attention to the world and yourself. This could be anything from savouring food and drink – really tasting the flavours, feeling the temperature and textures – to walking a new route and really paying attention to your surroundings – what you can see, hear and smell.

COLOUR

Give yourself a mindful break by filling this page with colour. Any colours you like and any pattern you like. As you go, focus on the different shades of the colours and the sensation of the pen/pencil/crayon/paintbrush as it moves across the paper. Notice how the colour settles on the page. Don't worry about the finished product, this is all about the process.

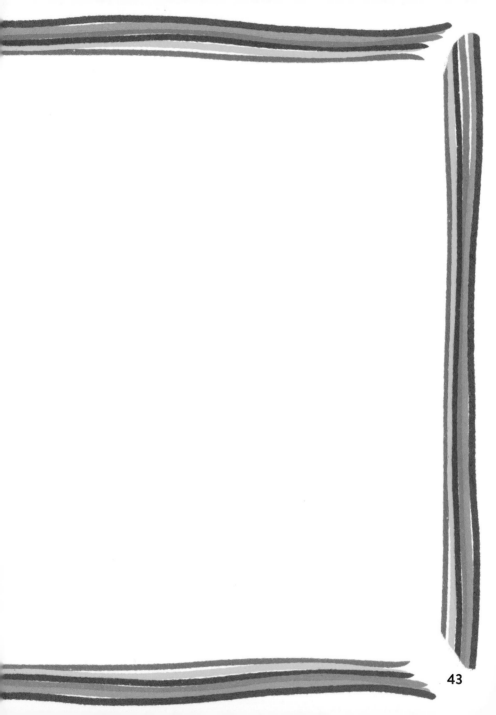

BEING WITH YOUR FEELINGS

This exercise – it's actually a form of mindfulness meditation – is about making space for the way that you're feeling right now. Rather that struggling with your emotions, you're being present with them, showing yourself that it is **OK** to experience them, whether you know why you're feeling this way or not.

1. Make yourself comfortable.

2. Take a couple of slow, deep breaths, then close your eyes.

3. Breathe normally and place your attention on the movement of air as you inhale and exhale.

4. See if you can allow whatever feelings you are currently experiencing to be with you right now – just as they are.

5. Name each emotion that you are feeling.

6. Accept that you are feeling this way. Acceptance isn't the same as liking. Rather it is about acknowledging that you can't control how you are feeling and you don't need to.

7. Recognize that these feelings are not trying to hurt you and they will pass.

8. Remind yourself that you are human and you are allowed to feel your feelings.

9. Whenever your mind wanders just notice that this has happened and where it's gone to and then gently bring your attention back to your breath and then back to your feelings.

10. Try to maintain this focus for a few minutes.

11. When you're ready to finish, open your eyes.

Having made space for and acknowledged your feelings, you can decide what you'd like to do now. Perhaps something from your self-care toolkit?

MOOD DIARY

Keeping a mood diary can help you become aware of how your feelings and mood change over time. Use the squares here to record your feelings for each day this week. You can use words, sentences, pictures or colours. You could even split the squares up into sections to represent the morning, afternoon and evening, as your mood could shift over the course of the day.

At the end of the week look back at your record and consider any patterns. Are there periods when you were struggling? Do you know what caused those moods? How might you help yourself during such times?

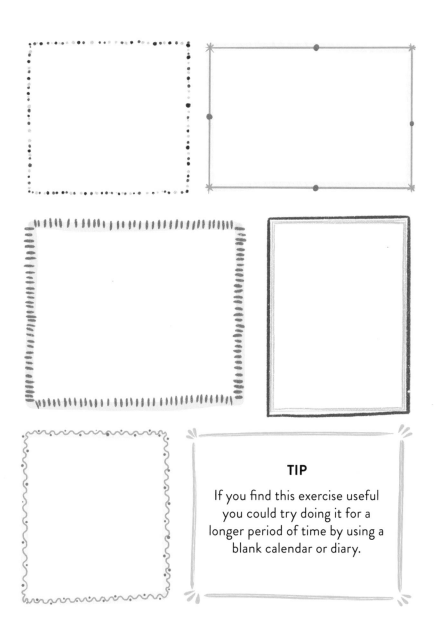

TIP

If you find this exercise useful you could try doing it for a longer period of time by using a blank calendar or diary.

SOMETIMES IT'S NOT YOU

Life doesn't always go to plan. Tough times come along. Good times come along. We don't always get to choose. And not feeling like you're in control can be difficult. That's understandable. But just recognizing when this is the case can help us to manage the situation better.

For example, it can put the brakes on some unhelpful automatic ways of thinking. Such as when something bad happens that's out of our control we can sometimes blame ourselves, because we might feel like if it's our fault then we at least have the power to stop it from happening again. The problem is that this can leave us feeling guilty and responsible for things that weren't our fault, and doesn't actually give us any more control. It can also encourage us to believe things about ourselves which are not true. For example, finding it tough during a worrying time might lead you to believe 'I can't deal with stress'. But maybe it was just a really stressful time.

When we don't feel in control it is important to be kind to ourselves and acknowledge how this is making us feel (flip back to 'Being With Your Feelings'). Talk about it with friends or family if you can, or there are help lines you can talk to (see the 'Resources' section at the back of the book).

ENJOY MORE

Let's get down to basics for a moment. Doing things we enjoy makes us happy. Doing more things we enjoy, in terms of variety and frequency, will give us more opportunities for happiness (within reason, of course – a life spent solely playing videogames might get a little repetitive). So far, so obvious, you might say. But there may be times when we find other things need our attention, and the activities we used to enjoy become temporarily forgotten. This is your opportunity to take a minute and make sure you're balancing your life the best you can.

First, make a list over the page (left-hand column) of things you enjoy doing – big and small.

For each of the things on your list, think about how often you get to do that activity. Is there something on the list that you could do today, tomorrow, next week? Research has shown that looking forward to things we enjoy can have a powerful, positive impact on our mood, so, once you've made a plan, put a reminder of it in your diary or on a sticky note so you can look forward to doing it

Next, look down your list again and consider what it is precisely that you enjoy about each activity. Is it fun, challenging, engaging, relaxing? Do you get a sense of achievement out of it? Is it something that you do with friends or on your own? How does it leave you feeling afterwards?

Once you have a sense of why you enjoy each activity on the list, and what you get out of it, have a think about what other activities might give you similar benefits. Make another list, this time in the right-hand column, of some ideas. You might not do them all but they'll be a reminder for those times when you fancy trying something different.

TIP

Is there anything on that list which on reflection you don't enjoy? Maybe you've noticed that it doesn't actually leave you feeling great afterwards or it's stuff that you feel you ought to enjoy because others do. Could you scale them back or cut them out?

I enjoy ...

I could try ...

_____

_____

_____

_____

_____

_____

_____

_____

_____

_____

_____

_____

FOCUS ON THE MUSIC

We're often surrounded by music, when we're shopping, on the bus, studying, hanging out with friends, but when was the last time you sat down and really *listened*, focussed your attention and actually made sense of the lyrics, picked out the beats and riffs? (Disclaimer: apologies if your answer to this is 'five minutes ago because music is my world and my record deal will be coming through next month, thank you very much'.)

As humans, we all respond to music – every culture around the world has developed its own music – and this can be a full mind-body experience: connecting with our emotions, altering our mood, making us want to dance and sing along. Different kinds of music, have different effects, of course, but this means that we can use music to energize us as well as relax us.

So, rescue music from being merely 'background' and give it the quality time it (and you!) deserves.

RECHARGE

How do you get your energy back? Different people need different things. Maybe you're someone who finds it energizing to be around other people or maybe you find it helps to take some time for yourself. In the same way, different people find different situations tiring. One person's fun crowd at a party can be another's endurance test and vice versa. And a lot of the time it's a bit of both.

What does your balance look like? Do you feel you get enough recharge time? If not, have a think about ways that you could work that into your daily schedule. Use the space below to write down your ideal day, making sure you leave some time to recharge.

7/11 BREATHING

Breathing exercises like this one can be very handy when you're feeling nervous or worried. The reason why they work so well is that when you're feeling worried, your body responds by increasing your heart rate, tensing your muscles and breathing faster. Your emotions can also begin to feel stronger. But when we choose to slow our breathing down, it sends a message to our brain to calm down and relax.

1. Find a quiet, safe space where you can sit, stand or lie comfortably.

2. If you're lying down, position your arms so that they aren't touching your sides and your chest has room to expand.

3. If you're sitting or standing, place both feet flat on the floor, roughly hip-width apart.

TIP

If it feels difficult to reach the count of 7 as you breathe in and 11 as you breathe out, try 5 in and 9 out instead, or as many as feels comfortable. The key is that the out breath is longer than the in breath as it's the out breath that sends the reassuring message to our brain that we can calm down.

4. As you breathe in count to 7.

5. Allow the air to flow in through your nose (or your mouth if that's easier) and fill your lungs, but don't force it. It should feel comfortable.

6. As you breathe out count to 11.

7. Once you get into a rhythm try to gently relax the muscles in your body. You could start with your shoulders – when we're stressed they're often one of the first to tense up.

8. If you can, take big deep breaths so your tummy expands. This 'belly breathing' helps you take relaxing deep breaths rather than shallow ones.

9. Keep repeating this process for a few minutes or until you feel your body and mind start to relax.

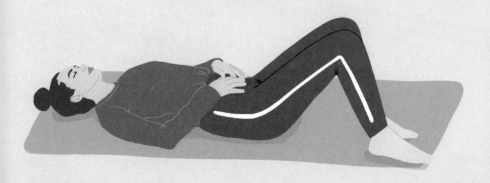

KEEPING GROUNDED

If you find yourself getting very worried or nervous in certain situations, such as before an exam or presentation, these techniques can help you in the moment to re-ground yourself. The 7/11 breathing exercise on the previous page is a great place to start, but there's more that you can do which uses this same idea of changing your behaviour to influence your feelings and thoughts.

When we're feeling worried, often our breathing speeds up, our heart starts racing and we may begin to sweat. This is commonly called the fight or flight response. Back in the day when our ancestors were facing dangerous threats from predators that might eat them this was pretty useful, as it essentially prepares our system for either fighting or running (notice how similar the physical symptoms are to those we experience when we exercise hard). But in our modern world, situations that we see as being very stressful can trigger the same response even when we are in no physical danger.

Like with the 7/11 breathing technique the strategies here are all about reassuring our brain that we are not in physical danger and that our body and mind don't need to be in this hyped up exercise-ready state.

1. Name the worry – use as many words as you can to describe the worry that you feel. The more words (written or spoken) the better. For more details on how to do this and why it works flip to 'Flood the Page' on page 98.

2. Use a distraction technique – focus on your senses. Taste mint-flavoured sugar-free gum or touch or cuddle something soft.

3. Repeat points 1 to 2 – it may take more than one go to feel the effects.

4. Remember to offer yourself compassion (see page 22). Challenging strong, instinctual feelings can be tough.

TIP

Research has shown that chewing sugar-free gum can actually help us to calm down. Our salivary response shuts down when we're frightened and so by chewing gum and getting our saliva going we're sending the message to our brain that we're not in a frightening situation.

DON'T FORGET THE SMALL STUFF

When you're feeling worried or overwhelmed, try asking yourself: what do I need right now? We're talking small, manageable things here, so the year-long holiday will just have to wait, I'm afraid.

- Is it a break?

- Is it a drink or a snack?

- Is it a chat with someone?

- Is it to have a moment by myself?

- Is it to get some fresh air?

- Is it to sit quietly with a breathing exercise or some music?

If you're not able to do that thing right then and there – maybe you're with family, on the bus or at school or college – think ahead to when you will have time and make a plan to do it then. Or maybe there's an alternative that would fit the situation? Even just a few deep breaths can feel soothing and help us acknowledge what's going on while doing something to put our wellbeing first.

POWER UP

Exercising helps us process thoughts and feelings, reduces stress and anxiety, improves concentration and focus, aids sleep, boosts memory and mood, increases our self-esteem, plus we get to enjoy a nice endorphin burst (our body's feel-good chemical).

There is no need to buy specialist gear or a gym membership that costs the same as a small mortgage. The beauty of it is that you get all these benefits whether you're competing at the Olympics or just enjoying a walk in the fresh air.

There are options for you to get your body moving whatever your ability, whether that is a short walk or taking the stairs instead of the lift, or a group activity like tennis, rounders or football. Lots of exercises can be adapted to be suitable for your own needs – you should be able to find lots of resources online to help you, including easy suggestions and video tutorials.

However you go about it, know that with every run, walk, cycle, skate, dance, swim, kick about, you're growing stronger from the inside out.

STRETCH OUT

For those times when a full-on yoga session just isn't going to happen, simply doing a few gentle stretches can work to release tension that's built up in your body, helping you to relax and destress.

We each hold tension in different places, so the first job is to locate where you store yours. Try moving and flexing the different parts of your body and pay attention to anywhere that feels tight or inflexible.

It's common to hold tension in our shoulders and neck – particularly if we've been working at a computer – so you could start off with these shoulder rolls. But do look online for stretches that suit you (flip to the 'Resources' section at the back of the book for some suggestions). Remember, do what feels right to you and don't overdo it. The stretches should feel like gentle pressure – they definitely shouldn't hurt!

1. Stand or sit up as straight as you can.

2. Take a few slow, deep breaths to help relax your body.

3. Roll your shoulders up, then back, then down in a fluid motion.

4. Repeat this movement about 10 times.

5. Then reverse it, rolling forward about 10 times.

CHANGING HABITS

Maybe you've decided you'd like to be in nature more, tweak your phone use or read more books. Changing our everyday habits can be tricky – they are habits, after all! But there are things you can do to give yourself a better chance at success.

1. **Think small**
    It can be tempting to try and change lots of things all at once but that can set us up for failure. Choosing something small and manageable means you're more likely to achieve that goal and with success comes the motivation to try more.

2. **Try it for a month**
    It can take 30 days to establish a new habit, so don't give up. After the 30 days it should become easier.

3. **Make it part of your routine**
    By connecting your new habit to something you already do, you're giving yourself a ready-made prompt. For instance, if you wanted to get more exercise, you could swap the bus for cycling or walking. Or if you're trying to avoid checking your phone at night, you could turn it off when you brush your teeth.

4. **Involve other people**
    This could be anything from joining a sports team to organizing a charity walk/run/cycle/whatever or even just telling your family or friends about your new goal. Involving others gives us extra motivation.

5. **Be prepared for slip ups**
    If making new habits was easy, we'd never break a new year's resolution! That means you almost certainly will slip up. You'll skip that run, reinstall that app, forget about that book. It's natural! The thing you want to avoid is allowing the inevitable slip ups to discourage you. Check out 'Failure is a Stupid Word' for more on this.

6. **Mentally reward yourself**
    Especially during those first 30 days. This is about giving yourself the time to mentally absorb that pat on the back every time you get a step closer to your goal. Let yourself bask in how good it feels. You did it!

... AND RELAX

This is a brilliantly simple and effective technique for when you want to relax. All you need is your imagination.

1. Close your eyes.

2. Take a couple of slow, deep breaths.

3. Think of somewhere relaxing and peaceful. It might be a memory of somewhere you've been before, or a picture you've seen, or an entirely imagined place.

4. Imagine entering this place. What textures can you feel beneath your feet? Look around you. What do you see? Can you hear any sounds? Is it warm or cool? Allow your mind to slowly explore the space.

5. You might find somewhere comfy to relax. Imagine the sensation of stopping there and being at peace in this world.

TIP

Try this technique next time
you're struggling to drift
off to sleep.

5-MINUTE ANTI-PROCRASTINATION BLITZ

If you're struggling with getting started on a new project, try this 5-minute blitz to get you moving again.

Choose one small thing that you've been meaning to do that you can do today. It might be putting away washing, replying to an email, writing that first paragraph of an essay, whatever it is make sure that it's just one thing and you can realistically complete it in five minutes (for bigger tasks select one tiny bit of it).

Set a timer on your phone for five minutes and get started. Keep focussed for the whole five minutes. When you're finished, take stock of what you've achieved.

FAILURE IS NOT 'THE END'

'Failure'. It sounds so final, doesn't it? 'It/I failed.' Full stop. Story over. The end.

Except it isn't the end, not by a long shot. In fact, most of the time it's just a necessary part of the process. We learn from failure and we all need to learn along the way to get where we want to be.

There is no athlete, director, artist, business person or anyone else for that matter who has achieved their goals without failing along the way. When you were a little kid learning to walk you fell over A LOT. But that didn't stop you. Your body and brain learned from all of those falls, and now look at you go!

Risking failure can be a scary business. When things don't go to plan it can bring us down. And that's totally fine and understandable. But it's not the end of the story. The plot will need a bit of tweaking and that can take bravery, but bravery is actually defined by failure: there's no bravery when you're sure of success. And just like when you were learning to walk, every bit of practice in bravery counts. So, failure isn't so much as 'The End' but 'Chapter Two'.

TIP

If you find yourself beating yourself up when you feel that you've failed at something, check out 'The Stories We Tell Ourselves' and 'Practice Compassion'.

JUST
FOR FUN

A few pages ago, you wrote a list of the things that you enjoy doing. Flip back to that page now and see if there are any activities on that list which you could categorize under 'just for fun'. We're talking things that won't make you more clever or fitter or a better person, like when you were a kid and you'd do things *just because you wanted to*. Maybe it's playing with a pet, watching repeats of your favourite movie, playing video games or fashioning woodland creatures out of Blu Tack – there's no judgement here!

If there's nothing on that list that quite fits the bill, you could think about whether there is anything you'd like to try in the future.

GROW
SOMETHING

There's something very special about watching a plant grow from a seed. Observing it change every day can be a mindful process, helping us to slow down and pay attention to the small things. There is also great satisfaction to be found in nurturing a tiny seed into a flourishing plant that you continue to care for.

You won't always get it right. You might over water it, under water, you might forget about it. The seed itself might not be healthy or the conditions might not be quite right. That's OK. It happens in nature all the time. An oak tree can create over 10 million acorns over its lifecycle and only a few of these will become fully grown trees. But if you keep going and try different seeds and different methods it will work in the end. And if it's a fruit or vegetable you'll have the chance to harvest the results. Nothing tastes as good as food that we've grown with our own two hands. And when you finally get to tuck in, don't forget to cast your mind back to that tiny seed and the extraordinary things it was capable of.

TIP

Seeds are often cheap to buy but you can also use seeds from your fruit and vegetable scraps, such as peppers, tomatoes, melons, avocados or herbs. Look online for advice on how to grow that particular plant as each one needs slightly different conditions.

TOMATO

PACK OF SEEDS

THERE IS NO SUCH THING AS PERFECT

There just isn't. Just like being happy all the time is not a thing, neither is being perfect. Because the problem with 'perfect' is that there isn't ever really an end to it. You might get 100% in a test, but could you have done it faster, revised less? You reach one goal but then the bar gets raised again.

It's not surprising that a lot of us feel the pressure to try to be perfect. Whether it's exam results or social media followers, we are often surrounded by rankings and judgement and the sense of unrealistic expectations. But we are not meant to be perfect. Not only is it impossible but life would be pretty boring if it were. Mistakes, flaws, imperfections, missteps, messiness: that's the brilliant, colourful, surprising real world that we live in.

How might you remind yourself that you don't need to be perfect? Scribble some ideas on the page opposite. Or you could try the exercise 'Make Something' on page 83 or have a look at 'Failure is Not the End' on page 74.

MAKE SOMETHING

Anything. As long as it's something real and tangible, and it can be a good idea to aim for something with an end result so you can get that sense of satisfaction when you've finished. It could be made out of clay, wool, wood, Lego. It might be a jigsaw or a picture you've drawn or coloured in.

Research has shown that engaging in creative activities helps focus the mind, boosts mood and reduces stress so it's the doing that counts.

It doesn't matter if it's rubbish. Maybe you were aiming for an Etsy-style mug and it's turned out more blobfish. Maybe you'll get better at it. Maybe you won't. It doesn't really matter. What matters is that you did that. You spent time, using your hands, or feet, or whatever, to create something. It wasn't there before and now it is. And while you were doing it, your body and mind were enjoying the benefits. That questionable mug/blobfish is now a testament to how you care about your wellbeing. And that's always mantelpiece worthy.

DANCE

We know that exercise and movement is good for us, but put it together with music and you get an instant mood-boosting effect like no other.

The instructions for this are pretty simple, too.

1. Compile an energetic and upbeat playlist.

2. Close curtains and lock doors if necessary.

3. Let yourself go.

CURIOSITY

This is another simple one.

Feed it.

Follow it.

When we're young we spend a lot of time learning new things – in school, college, at work. Sometimes we find it interesting, sometimes not so much. All knowledge is valuable stuff, but we shouldn't just leave our curiosity in the classroom.

Being curious and discovering new ideas can boost self-confidence and self-esteem, helps build a sense of purpose and connects us with others. What's not to like?!

Is there a subject you've always wanted to know more about? Wondered how that whatsit over there works? Or why that happens? Or what happened then?

You could watch Ted Talks online. Read books and articles. Ask questions. Try it out for yourself. Take in one side of an argument and then the other. Make up your own mind. Change it. Change it again.

This world we live in is a brilliant, strange, complex and astonishing place. What are you into?

WALKING THROUGH IT

We know our thoughts and feelings affect us physically. For example, when we're upset we might cry, when we're stressed our heart rate can go up. And the opposite is true, too. Remember in '7/11 Breathing' and 'Keeping Grounded' when you used behaviours such as breathing, exercise and sugar-free chewing gum to help you calm down? This connection between our minds and bodies is also one of the reasons why exercise is good for us mentally as well as physically (see 'Power Up' for more about the benefits).

But you don't always have to break a sweat to make the most of it, and this is particularly true when you need to gain clarity on a problem or come up ideas and think creatively. In these cases walking can be just what's needed.

Aim for somewhere relatively quiet where you roughly know the route so you don't have to check it (a park can be a good option). If it's hard to find somewhere quiet, you could bring relaxing music with you so you aren't too distracted. If you can do it in nature that's even better (see 'Be at One with Nature' for why). Walk at a pace that's comfortable for you and just allow your mind to do its thing.

BE AT ONE
WITH NATURE

Being in nature, somewhere there are trees, plants, grass, animals or water, has been shown to have a powerful effect on our wellbeing. Our blood pressure and stress levels drop, our immune system gets a boost and other lovely things happen in our brains and bodies to help us relax and feel good.

We get some of these benefits even when we're not paying attention, but you can get some extra goodness by doing this simple mindfulness-based exercise.

You can do this in a garden or park, or just as well with a tree on the pavement or a plant growing in the cracks of a wall. And if you can't be outside, house plants, pets or even looking out of a window are other options.

1. Choose something to focus your attention upon. It might be a flower, or a leaf, or a pond.

2. Take a couple of slow, deep breaths.

3. Get close up.

4. Notice its outline, and the different colours and variations in shade.

5. Look even closer. What shapes can you see? What details?

6. If you can touch it, how does it feel?

7. Does it have a smell?

8. When you're ready to finish take another couple of deep breaths.

TIP

When you've finished the exercise, you could make a sketch of what you were looking at here as a reminder of the power of nature.

SLEEP

Good quality sleep helps support all sorts of things, from physical wellbeing to brain functioning and emotional health, and it's been shown that teenagers actually need more than adults – about 8 to 9 hours on average is a good goal.

Most of us don't get enough sleep, though, so if you're one of those who struggles to drift off, give the tips below a try.

- **Switch off:** The light from our screens has been shown to interfere with sleep. Aim for at least 30 minutes of screen-free time before going to bed. You could use a blue light filter or night mode on your screen in the evening to help you feel sleepy. You could read a book for 30 minutes or use a mindfulness app or audiobook to help you relax.

- **Exercise:** Regular physcial activity helps you sleep more soundly. See 'Power Up' for inspiration.

- **Cut the caffeine:** Particularly in the 4 hours before bed, but the less you have during the day the better. Caffeine can stop you from falling asleep and messes with the quality of sleep even once you're snoozing.

- **Create a sleep sanctuary:** You're aiming for a room that's dark, cool, quiet and comfortable. Have a look at 'Your Sanctuary' for more tips.

- **Set up a routine:** Going to bed and waking at roughly the same time every day, even at weekends, helps your body clock stay reliable and helps you drift off.

- **Talk through any problems:** Try talking worries through with a family member or friend during the day. You could also try writing down your worries before going to bed (see 'Park It').

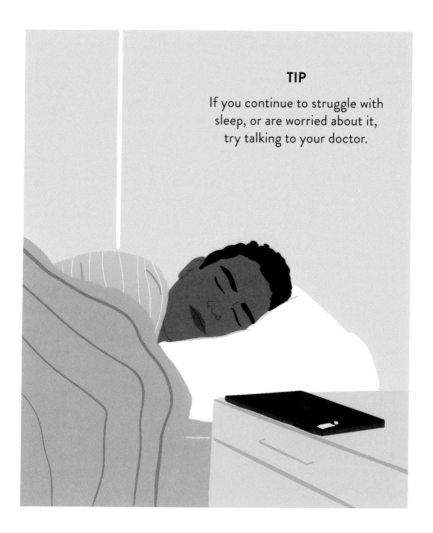

TIP

If you continue to struggle with sleep, or are worried about it, try talking to your doctor.

PARK IT

Do you find your brain whirring with everyday worries or a nagging to-do list? You might find that it gets in the way of being able to focus on a task or feeling truly relaxed. This exercise is one strategy that you can use to quieten the whirr.

1. Find a safe, quiet space and just notice the thoughts that are going through your mind.

2. As you notice each one, write them down on the following pages.

3. When you feel like you've got enough of them down on paper, close this book or turn the page.

4. Consciously decide to park them here. You're not ignoring them. You're just going to leave them here. Set a time to revisit these worries, perhaps wait 24 hours and come back to them to see how you feel.

You could try this exercise before doing some of the relaxation and mindfulness techniques in this book, such as 'Focus' on page 16.

TIP

Some people find it helpful to
write their worries down on bits of
paper and then rip them up.

FLOOD THE PAGE

Another technique for managing worries is to 'flood' a piece of paper with them. This is when you write (or speak) about your worries in as many words as you can. It doesn't matter what words you use or how strong they might seem, and you don't have to write in sentences.

Just the act of releasing them, emptying them out of your mind and onto the paper, has been shown to reduce anxiety and stress levels. In fact, studies have shown that the more words you use, the more levels tend to drop, and this was the case even when people didn't initially expect the technique to work.

Next time you're feeling worried or anxious, use the pages here to try it for yourself.

DE-STRESS
SUPPORT PLAN

Got something stressful coming up? Use the space here to make a plan now for how you can take care of yourself. Think about things that will help support you. Make sure that you have something every day that's just for you. You might want to make a note of some of the exercises in this book that you find helpful and take a look back at your 'Self-Care Toolkit'.

CONNECTIONS

Humans are social animals and our relationships can bring us a lot of happiness, whether that's with our friends, family, sports team or whomever.

Different people need different amounts and types of connection so think about what brings you happiness in your relationship. Strengthen your current relationships with kindness and gratitude. If you'd like to build new ones, consider what opportunities might be available such as joining a club or class. Or if meeting new people sounds daunting are there safe online spaces you could try?

WRITE IT FORWARD

What words of encouragement and support could you give yourself when times get tough? Use the space here to write a letter to your future self.

If you're stuck for ideas, you could cast your mind back to difficult periods from your past. What did you learn from those experiences? What helped you get through? How did you take care of yourself? What would you like to do differently in the future? What words of comfort would you have found reassuring?

You could keep a copy of this note in your 'Self-Care Toolkit' (see page 24) so it's right there ready for when you need it.

TIP

Some difficult experiences can affect you for a long time. They may affect how you think or feel, or how you act. If you're worried, talk to a trusted adult, like a parent/carer or a doctor.

YOUR SANCTUARY

If you have a space that's your own – your bedroom, for example, or a particular spot such as your bed or desk – think now about how you feel when you're in that space. Are you relaxed and happy? Or tense and uncomfortable? Do you want to spend time there? What is it about that space that makes you feel this way?

Think about the purpose of that space. Is it for relaxation or study? What things do you have on show? What colours are there? Do they feel like they support that purpose? Do they support you? Does the level of light work? Is it cluttered? How is the room arranged? Is there anything that you'd like to change?

Even small changes can have a big effect and you don't need a full room makeover to make a difference. Moving furniture around, decorating with photos that make you smile, adding a pot plant to a desk or a cosy blanket to your bed can all help make a space feel more like your own.

ALWAYS ON?

On average, adults spend over 4 hours a day looking at screens, and for teenagers it's over 7. Given that your average waking day is only around 15 hours that's one serious relationship.

There's nothing inherently good or bad about our devices and they're often a normal part of people's everyday life, but it's important to recognize that they can also have a significant impact on our thoughts, feelings and behaviours. Without realizing it we can give our phones and the content we view through them a lot of power. Taking an honest look at how we use our phones (for most of us it is phones, but also think about tablets and computers) means we can take that power back.

- How many hours a day do you spend on your phone?

- How do you use that time? Are you watching videos, playing games, posting on social media, chatting to friends, checking emails, scrolling through feeds?

- For each of those uses, consider: how do you feel while you're doing it? How do you feel afterwards?

- How many times, on average, do you check your phone each day (or more likely, hour)?

- What time of day do you first check your phone?

- What motivates you to pick up your phone (other than when you hear a notification)?

- How do you react when you hear a notification?

- How does it feel when you are without your phone?

You might not feel that you want to change anything about your screen use, but if you do, you could think about changing your notification settings, having periods when you don't check your phone. You could even try turning it off for a bit! Uninstall the apps that make you feel rubbish, perhaps look for others that you'd enjoy more. If you've noticed that you turn to your phone out of boredom think about things that you could do instead. Maybe read a book, watch your favourite TV show or cook up a storm in the kitchen.

Let's face it, it's not always easy to change our habits, so don't be surprised if you uninstall and reinstall those troublesome apps more than a few times. You could also check out 'Changing Habits' for some tips on how to make the changes stick.

DON'T FALL FOR THE LIES

We all know that social media is not the most truthful place. Photos are altered and filtered to within an inch of their lives, posts are often more about how people want to be seen rather than how they are, and 'facts' can be anything but.

But even when we *know* what we're seeing isn't real it can still have a nasty habit of encouraging us to compare how we see ourselves and our lives (often focussing on our perceived flaws) with what we see on the screen. And we can feel like we have to join in, that we have to edit ourselves, too. We can end up absorbing the lies and believing that we are not acceptable as we are. This can affect our self esteem and mood, increasing our worry and even our ability to concentrate.

That's not to say it's all bad. Social media can be a great way to stay in touch with people, find out what's going on in the world, share our interests and find new ones. We just have to keep hold of a healthy dose of reality, as well as a wary eye on how it's affecting us, and remind ourselves that we can choose who and what we let onto our phone.

Think now about who you follow on social media. What do you get out of following them? How do they make you feel about yourself? Think also about what you post and why. Test out some changes and see what difference they make. You could use the 'Mood Diary' to keep track (see page 46).

LAUGH MORE

Earlier in the book we talked about doing more things you enjoy because it makes you happy. Well here's another that'll probably seem blindingly obvious. Because, laughter = happy, naturally. Actually, the equation is a little more complicated than that because laughter isn't just fun, it actually affects our mood and overall wellbeing.

Laughter ...

- reduces physical tension, making you feel less stressed

- triggers the release of endorphins, our body's feel-good chemicals

- can strengthen our relationships with others

- helps us shift perspective, so we can see things in a different light

How might you bring more laughter into your life? YouTube is filled with stand-up comedy clips or maybe your next movie choice could be a comedy. It turns out that we're 30 times more likely to laugh when we're with others, so think about involving some friends or family.

WIN WIN KINDNESS

Research has shown that carrying out acts of kindness can boost our sense of wellbeing and happiness, as well as showing those who we're helping that they are cared about.

Over the next week keep an eye out for opportunities to offer people support.

It might be holding open a door for an elderly person or giving a family member a hug. You could do a household chore unasked, write a thank you note, ask someone how they're doing – and really mean it (for tips, check out 'The Art of Listening' over the page)!

Don't forget to enjoy the feel-good afterglow that you get from helping someone out! It might help make it more of a habit.

TIP

Caring for others shouldn't come at the expense of caring for yourself. If you notice that you're someone who's always doing things for others, try and take some time for yourself – 'Self-Care Toolkit' has some ideas to get you started.

THE ART OF LISTENING

Or should that be the 'science' of listening? Because there is a science to it, and while many of us may assume that listening is easy, 'active listening' – listening so that someone feels truly heard – takes more effort than you think. Active listening is where we are fully focussed on hearing and understanding what's being said to us. We're not distracted by our own thoughts or planning our reply. And we make sure that the other person is aware that we are listening.

Next time you think a friend might need it, try out some of the following active listening techniques:

- Show that you're fully present and interested. That means making regular eye contact – and no checking your phone!

- Avoid jumping in. You can show you're listening without having to say much. The occasional 'uh huh' or nodding your head can be enough.

- Try using open questions (questions that encourage more than a one word or one sentence answer), such as 'What happened then?' 'What was that like?'

- Don't be tempted to fix it. It's natural to want to help people solve their problems, but sometimes they just want to share and be understood.

- Be respectful. Consider what it might be like to be them. Something that might not seem like a big deal to you, might feel huge to them.

- Beware of 'story-stealing'. When we hear someone tell us a story we often think of something similar that happened to us and want to share that too. That can make for a good chat, but when you're trying to listen actively it can mean the other person doesn't feel heard.

- Pay attention to how something is being said as well as what is being said. Maybe someone is saying that they're fine when their body language says otherwise. You can then use open questions to give them the chance to open up if they want to.

THE POWER OF NO

It's great saying yes to things, but in some situations we need to feel able to take a pause, think about what is important to us and actually make a conscious choice about what we *really* want.

This isn't about holding yourself back, taking a negative view on things, or feeling like we can't be spontaneous. It's about listening to your gut, knowing what's right for you and when it's right. It's about developing confidence in that inner compass which tells you that you don't have to go along with others when you feel the right direction for you is different. Because, sometimes the positive answer is no – thanks, but no.

Use the space opposite to think about some of things you would have liked to say no to, and how you could have politely turned them down.

NO!

NO!

THANK YOU ...

Use the pages here to write a thank you note to each of the things in your life that you feel grateful for. Think about what each one offers you and why you feel grateful for them.

Regularly practising gratitude like this can help us to feel more content and deal better with the stresses that life throws our way. You can also turn back to these pages when you think you could do with a reminder.

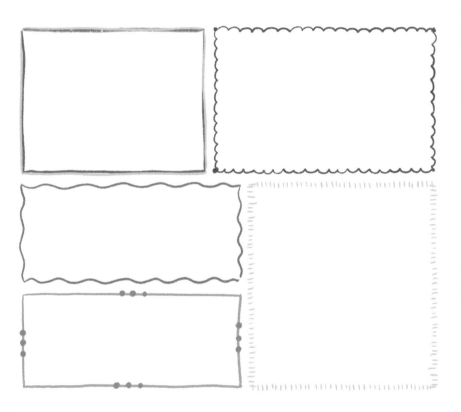

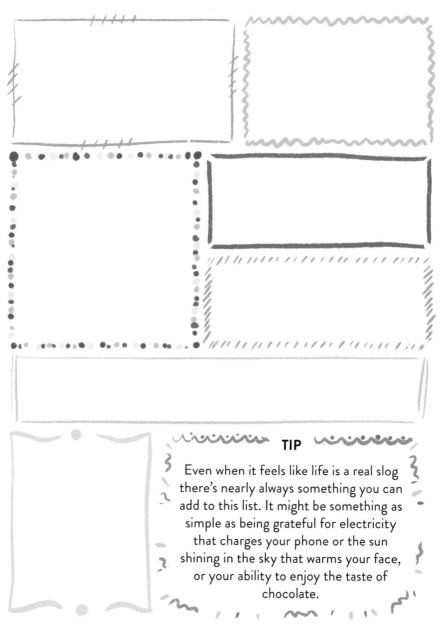

TIP

Even when it feels like life is a real slog there's nearly always something you can add to this list. It might be something as simple as being grateful for electricity that charges your phone or the sun shining in the sky that warms your face, or your ability to enjoy the taste of chocolate.

POSITIVE
AFFIRMATIONS

Positive affirmations are short, powerful statements you can use to motivate yourself and others around you. They can create balance in your day and remind you what is important in your life.

There is no one way to use positive affirmations. You may want to say them out loud in front of a mirror, write them down in a journal, or just repeat the words in your head. Whether you do them when you wake up, before you go to sleep, in the shower or on your way to school, it is important to do them at the same time every day to form a habit.

Below are some examples to inspire you. Positive affirmations work best when they feel natural, like something you would say to a friend.

- I am enough.

- I am allowed to take up space.

- I am allowed to make mistakes; they don't define me.

- I have the power to create change.

- I speak to myself with kindness.

- I consider other people's feelings.

- I am good at helping others to [fill in the blank].

GRADE YOUR WORRY

This is a simple technique that helps you to give you a little bit of perspective about your worries.

Take some time to think about the thing that is causing you the most worry. Grade the worry from 0 to 10 – converting what you're feeling into a number uses the rational, thinking centres of our brain. By giving it a number we're in a better position to observe the fear rather than just being in it. Once you've graded it, choose a number on the scale that you feel would be OK – it doesn't have to be 0 just something manageable for right now. Next, use the 7/11 breathing exercise for a minute or two until you reach that number.

Use the space here to jot down your worries and the number you have given them.

RESOURCES

You can find additional resources on the Mind website at:
mind.org.uk/information-support/for-children-and-young-people

For support and advice in your area, find your local Mind
at mind.org.uk/localmind

If you are feeling overwhelmed or need a listening ear,
we recommend contacting Samaritans.
Phone: 116 123
24 hours a day, 365 days a year

You can also find useful resources for mental and physical
help on the NHS website. www.nhs.uk